CANADA

the culture

Bobbie Kalman

The Lands, Peoples, and Cultures Series

Crabtree Publishing Company

The Lands, Peoples, and Cultures Series

Created by Bobbie Kalman

To Jacqui Keeping
for a song

Editor-in-Chief
Bobbie Kalman

Writing team
Bobbie Kalman
Janine Schaub
David Schimpky
Lynda Hale
Tammy Everts

Editors
David Schimpky
Lynda Hale
Tammy Everts

Illustrations
Antoinette "Cookie" DeBiasi

Computer design and layout
Antoinette "Cookie" DeBiasi
Lynda Hale
Campbell Creative Services

Separations and film
Book Art Inc.

Printer
Worzalla Publishing

Special thanks to: James Campbell and the Weir Foundation, The Canadian Native Arts Foundation, Charlottetown Festival, Cirque du Soleil, Famous People Players, Industry, Science and Technology Canada, The MuchMusic Network, The National Archives of Canada, The National Ballet of Canada, Tamara Jones, The National Ballet School of Canada, The National Gallery of Canada, The Ontario Ministry of Tourism and Recreation, The Oshawa Folk Arts Council, The Shaw Festival, The Stratford Festival, Sullivan Films, Theatre Beyond Words, and The Young People's Theatre

Photographs

Canadian Native Arts Foundation: page 6
Canapress/Ray Giguere: page 27 (top)
Canapress/Rusty Kennedy: page 27 (bottom right)
Charlottetown Festival/Anne of Green Gables: page 15 (bottom)
Cirque du Soleil/Al Seib: cover, title page, pages 8, 9 (both)
Marc Crabtree: pages 5 (circle), 10 (top, middle), 13 (all), 24
Famous People Players: page 17 (bottom)
Ken Faris: page 30
Industry, Science and Technology, Canada: pages 5 (bottom left), 19 (bottom), 27 (bottom left), 28, 29
James Kamstra: page 25 (bottom)
Diane Payton Majumdar: pages 10 (bottom), 11 (bottom right), 20 (bottom left), 27 (inset)
Bob Mansur: page 23

MuchMusic Network: page 19 (top)
National Archives of Canada/C-001111: page 5 (top)
National Ballet of Canada/D. Street: page 12
National Gallery of Canada/Timothy Hursley: page 25 (top)
National Gallery of Canada/Michael Snow: page 21
Ontario Ministry of Tourism and Recreation: page 22
Shaw Festival/David Cooper: page 15 (top)
Stratford Festival/David Cooper: page 14
Sullivan Films/Road to Avonlea: page 18
Theatre Beyond Words: page 16
Tourism Saskatchewan: page 31
Weir Collection, Queenston, Ontario: *Sketch for the Jack Pine*: page 20 (top), *Early Canadian Settler*: page 20 (bottom right)
Young People's Theatre/Tom Sandler: page 17 (top)

Published by
Crabtree Publishing Company

350 Fifth Avenue	360 York Road, RR 4,	73 Lime Walk
Suite 3308	Niagara-on-the-Lake,	Headington
New York	Ontario, Canada	Oxford OX3 7AD
N.Y. 10118	L0S 1J0	United Kingdom

Cataloguing in Publication Data

Kalman, Bobbie, 1947-
    Canada: the culture

(Lands, Peoples, and Cultures Series)
Includes index.
ISBN 0-86505-219-0 (library bound) ISBN 0-86505-299-9 (pbk.)
This book looks at the music, dance, traditions, architecture, theater, sports, and arts that make up Canada's culture.

1. Canada - Civilization - Juvenile literature. 2. Multiculturalism - Canada - Juvenile literature.* I. Title. II. Series.

FC95.4.K35 1993   j971
F1021.2.K35 1993

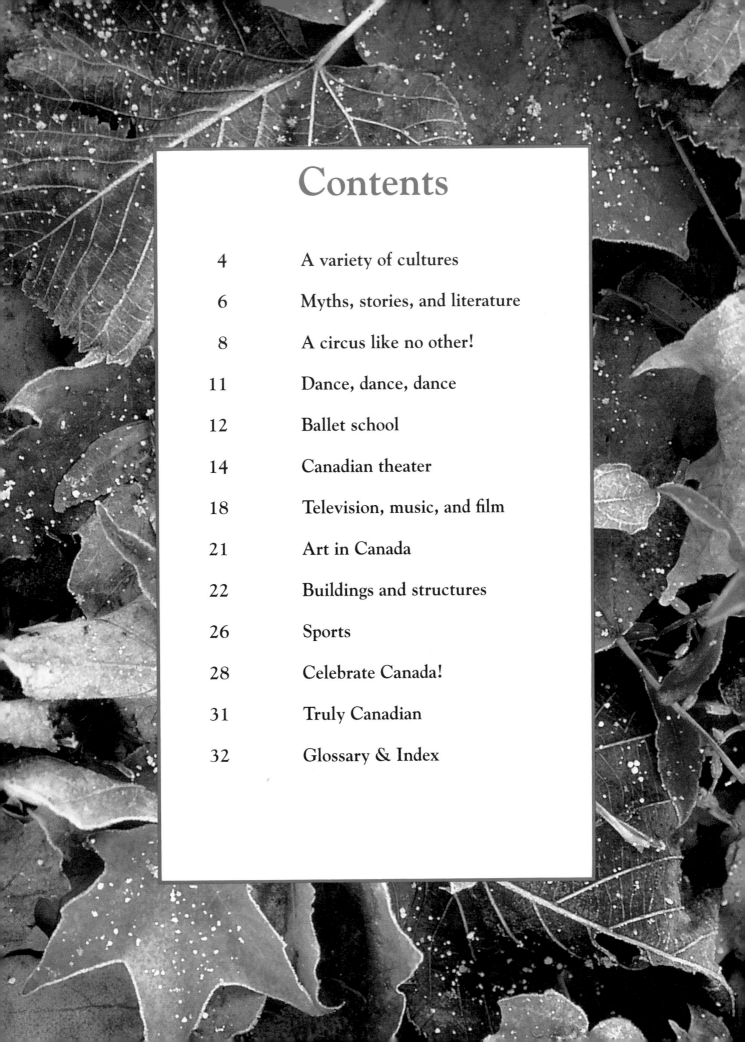

Contents

🦋 A variety of cultures 🦋

Culture is the way people live. It is the food they eat, the clothes they wear, the stories they tell or write, the buildings they build, the dances they perform, the music they enjoy, the religious beliefs they follow, and the sports they play or watch. Culture also includes customs and traditions such as celebrations and festivals.

A mixed heritage

Canada's culture started with the artwork, songs, dances, and stories of the Native peoples, who have lived in North America for thousands of years. It includes the way of life of the French Canadians, the first permanent European settlers. The British came one hundred years after the French and had the greatest influence on Canadian culture.

For many years, British culture was the main culture in Canada. Later, immigrants came from all over the world. Their contributions are many. Their creativity has influenced theater, music, literature, art, architecture, food, and dress.

South of the border

The culture of Canada has also been influenced by its neighbor, the United States. Favorite television programs, music, and many fads originate south of the border.

Support for culture

In recent years, Canadians have begun to realize the importance of maintaining their own distinct culture. The Canadian government supports its cultural industry with grants of money so that Canadian literature, music, art, and theater will continue to thrive in Canada. Many tourists visit Canada's cities and towns to enjoy the cultural attractions they offer.

Canada's culture is unique because it is a blend of many cultures. Canadians respect and cherish the ways of life of all its peoples.

(above) The traditional ways of French Canadians, such as blessing the children on New Year's Day, have been preserved in the art of Edmond-Joseph Massicotte.
(below left) Colorful embroidery is a popular form of Inuit art.
(below right) Caribbean festivals are celebrated in several Canadian cities.

🎭 Myths, stories, and literature 🎭

Every country in the world has **myths**, legends, and stories that people read or tell one another. Myths are ancient tales that may use fictional characters and situations to teach truths about life. Long ago, myths and legends taught values such as courage and honor and explained the mysteries of nature.

A Native tradition

Storytelling is an important Native tradition. For thousands of years, Native children were educated by listening to stories told by their elders. Sometimes storytelling was accompanied by dancing to the beat of a drum. The following story is based on an Ojibwa tale. It offers an explanation of how the earth came to be.

How the world was made

Long ago the earth was covered by a great sea. It was home to swimming mammals, fish, birds, and reptiles. High above them in the heavens the Sky Woman lived all alone.

To make her happy, the Great Spirit sent a companion, but the companion left. Soon after, the Sky Woman gave birth to twins who were not at all alike. They fought and finally destroyed each other, and the Sky Woman was alone again. The Great Spirit then sent another companion and, as before, the companion left.

The water creatures felt sorry that the Sky Woman was lonely and wanted her to come down and join them. They persuaded a giant turtle to offer his back as a resting place. The Sky Woman accepted the offer. Once settled, she asked the animals to dive down into the water and bring up some dirt from the bottom of the ocean.

The animals wanted to please the Sky Woman. The beaver was the first to dive deep into the sea. Soon he surfaced, out of breath but with no soil. The otter and marten each took a turn but returned to the surface empty-handed.

1. Robert Munsch

2. Lucy Maud Montgomery

3. Margaret Laurence

4. Stephen Leacock

5. Robert Service

6. Margaret Atwood

Finally, the muskrat volunteered. The other creatures laughed at him. They doubted that this small animal was any match for the task, but the little muskrat wanted to try. Down, down he went. He did not surface for a long time. The others became very worried. Just when they had given up hope for the return of their friend, the muskrat floated to the surface, close to death. Clutched in his tiny paws was a small bit of soil.

The Sky Woman painted the turtle's back with this soil. She breathed upon the soil, and it began to grow until it became a huge island. The Ojibwa people call this land "The Island of the Great Turtle." Other people call it North America.

(opposite page) The Canadian Native Arts Foundation (CNAF) is a national organization that provides assistance to Native youths for education and training in the arts. The CNAF developed the Canadian Native Dance Theatre, which presented a stage performance of the story you have just read. Called **In the Land of Spirits,** *it begins with the creation of "The Island of the Great Turtle" and ends in modern times. The performance combines traditional Native dances with classical ballet movements.*

From stories to books

When European settlers came to Canada, they brought their own storytelling traditions. Folk tales were very popular. People entertained one another by telling exciting stories. The story of a giant lumberjack named Paul Bunyan has its origins in a French-Canadian folk tale. Today, storytelling is not as much a part of Canadian life as it once was. Most of today's stories can be found in books.

Canadian writers

Canada has many famous writers and books. Stephen Leacock is remembered for his witty tales of early twentieth-century life in Ontario. The well-known "Anne of Green Gables" books, which follow the life of a spunky red-headed girl in Prince Edward Island, were written by Lucy Maud Montgomery. A poet named Robert Service wrote poems about the land and people of the Canadian Arctic. The works of Margaret Laurence and Margaret Atwood focus on the world as seen through the eyes of women. Young children are big fans of Robert Munsch, whose funny stories have made him famous.

♟ A circus like no other! ♟

"*C'est la vie*" means "that's life," and French Canadians know how to celebrate it! They express their cultural pride through a wide variety of arts. Even though French Canadians are surrounded by an English-speaking culture, they prefer their own music, films, literature, and theater. A good example of French Canada's culture is *Cirque du Soleil* or "Circus of the Sun." Based in Montreal, Quebec, it is like no other circus in the world!

Under the big top

The lights burst with color as the music builds. The crowd, nestled beneath the big blue and yellow circus tent, gasps as the trapeze artist flies overhead. He is so close that the audience can see beads of perspiration on his forehead!

Cirque du Soleil is a theater production and circus all in one. It is unique because there are no animals in its acts; all the performers are human.

A great deal of preparation goes into a show. The performers spend months rehearsing their parts. Musicians and light technicians create the right sound and light. Costume makers sew bright costumes. The result is unforgettable. Color, light, music, and drama are combined with traditional circus acts such as juggling, tightrope walking, and trapeze. This wonderful traveling show thrills and excites audiences throughout North America, Europe, and Japan.

Circus school

The *École Nationale de Cirque* is a special school in Montreal that works with *Cirque du Soleil* to train acrobats, trapeze artists, dancers, and actors. Students from all over the world come to this school to learn circus arts. Many of the graduates become *Cirque du Soleil* performers.

One of the Cirque du Soleil *performances is called* **Saltimbanco,** *which means "street performer" in old Italian. This high-energy production keeps audiences breathless.*

Cross-cultural festivals, which are held in many Canadian cities, highlight the different dancing styles of Canadians. Colorful Caribbean costumes (top), Ukrainian dancers (middle), and high-energy African-Canadian performances (below) can all be found at these festivals.

Dance, dance, dance

Canadians love to dance. They dance at weddings and birthday parties. They move to the rhythm of music at restaurants and night clubs. Babies start dancing almost as soon as they can walk. Just turn on some music, and they wiggle and wave their arms. Many children start dancing lessons at an early age. When they reach high school, dancing becomes a favorite school activity.

Cultural dancing

Canadians also express their heritage through dance. The Native peoples of Canada use dance as a part of religious ceremonies. The dances have many purposes: healing the sick, celebrating a successful hunt, or praying to the spirits. Singing and a steady drum beat accompany the dancing.

Ancient Asian dances, the happy stepping of a jig, and the leaps of a lively polka are all part of Canadian dance. Children explore their heritage by learning the dances of their cultural groups.

A performing art

Dance performances can be seen throughout Canada. Ballet, tap, jazz, and modern dance are all popular. Audiences are thrilled by the performances of Canadian ballet legends such as Karen Kain and Veronica Tennant. Musical plays also allow dancers to show off their talents.

(below left) Many Canadian children enjoy taking lessons in tap, jazz, and ballet.
(below right) This type of Indian dancing is called **Bharata Natyam.** *The movements represent different human emotions.*

🩰 Ballet school 🩰

Ballet is a beautiful and popular form of dance. Ballet companies tour the country presenting traditional works such as *Swan Lake* and *The Nutcracker* as well as ballets that are performed to modern music. One of the more famous troupes, the National Ballet of Canada, has earned international praise for its performances.

Ballet dancers begin their training as children. The National Ballet School of Canada, located in the city of Toronto, provides training for many future dancers.

Audition time

Ten-year-old Tamara was nervous because she was about to audition for the National Ballet School. She was just one of a thousand children trying out in twenty cities across Canada. Students from other countries also auditioned by sending in videotapes. Tamara had always dreamed of learning to be a dancer at the famous school. She wondered what it would be like to have some of the world's finest young dancers as schoolmates.

One of a few

Several weeks after the audition, Tamara's mother gave her the good news. She had been invited to attend the National Ballet School's July summer program. Tamara knew that if she worked very hard she might be fortunate enough to be chosen to live and study at the ballet school in the fall.

Leaving home to dance

Tamara's dream came true, and in September she began her fifth-grade program at the National Ballet School. She was amazed by all the things her new school had to offer. The ballet school had nine studios, a laboratory, classrooms, and a residence. Along with the teachers and dance instructors, there were physiotherapists and doctors in case a student was injured. There was even a famous dancer called an "artist-in-residence" working at the school.

A ballet school day

Each morning Tamara begins her classes at 8:45 and is seldom finished before 5:30 in the afternoon. She studies subjects such as French, music, math, and art history. Besides taking these classes, she dances two hours in the morning and spends another two hours in the afternoon swimming or doing other kinds of physical exercise. In the evening she has supervised study time at the school's residence, her new home.

After Tamara completes ballet school, she can choose to go to university or pursue another career. Tamara, however, dreams of becoming a successful ballet performer just like legendary dancer Karen Kain, a National Ballet School graduate.

Karen Kain is one of the world's great dancers. She has won many awards for her bold and original dancing style.

(above) While living in residence, Tamara eats meals with her friends.
(top right) Practice makes perfect! A major part of every day is dedicated to dance.
(below) Tamara participates in a game to learn about money in her social studies class.

🎭 Canadian theater 🎭

Imagine you are a young Canadian living in a small city in the year 1906. The residents of your town are very excited because an acting company is coming to perform. As a treat, your parents are taking you to see the performance. The day finally arrives. You sit in the theater, waiting for the curtain to rise. The play is about to begin!

Before the 1930s, American, British, and French theater companies toured Canada, putting on plays in cities and towns. These groups were so successful and famous that Canadian performers and playwrights had difficulty competing with them. Thanks to many talented and creative Canadians, however, theater is now thriving in Canada. Big cities such as Toronto, Ottawa, Montreal, and Vancouver have several theaters that showcase the talent of Canadian actors, dancers, and musicians. Even small towns have live theater. People travel from faraway countries to attend theater performances in Canada.

Charlottetown Festival

In the summer of 1965, the first production of the musical *Anne of Green Gables* was performed in Charlottetown, Prince Edward Island. This musical play is based on Lucy Maud Montgomery's novel. *Anne* was a big hit and has been shown in London, New York, and Japan.

Today *Anne of Green Gables* is performed at the Charlottetown Festival every year, along with other Canadian musicals. Many young Japanese couples flock to Prince Edward Island to get married in the province where Anne was supposed to have lived.

Stratford Festival

In 1953 Canada's first professional theater began in a tent! Located in Stratford, Ontario, this festival has become famous for its productions of plays written by William Shakespeare. In fact, the town is named after Shakespeare's birthplace in England! The tents disappeared years ago. Today the plays are performed in three large theaters.

Shaw Festival

The Shaw Festival produces the plays of Irish playwright George Bernard Shaw and other works written during the period in which Shaw lived. These plays include musicals, mysteries, dramas, and comedies. The Shaw acting company, the second largest in North America, performs in the historic town of Niagara-on-the-Lake, Ontario. By 1973 the Shaw Festival had become so popular that its two theaters were not enough to seat the large audiences. The Festival Theatre, which seats 850 people, was then built. It was officially opened by Queen Elizabeth II.

(left) Every season a number of William Shakespeare's plays, such as **The Tempest,** *are showcased in Stratford.*
(opposite page top) Bernard Shaw's **Pygmalion** *was a popular performance at the Shaw Festival.*
(opposite page bottom) Live theater is thriving across Canada, from British Columbia to this production of **Anne of Green Gables** *in Charlottetown, Prince Edward Island.*

Theatre Beyond Words

Have you ever seen a **mime** performance? Mime is a type of acting in which no one speaks. The story is told through facial expressions and body movements. Theatre Beyond Words is a theater group that combines the art of mime with colorful costumes, exciting music, and creative masks. It is famous for its Potato People plays, which are about the adventures of a loveable potato family. The Potato People performances are like living cartoons.

Famous People Players

Toronto is home to a very special group of performers called the Famous People Players. Their performances use a technique called **black-light theater**. The actors, dressed in black from head to toe, move large, colorful puppets.

A special light shines on the stage, illuminating the puppets while the actors remain invisible. The result is a beautiful, humorous, and unique theater experience. All the actors in Famous People Players are physically or mentally challenged. The group was started in 1974 by a woman named Diane Dupuy. Her dream was to show the world the abilities of people who were once called "disabled."

Banff Festival of the Arts

Nestled in the Rocky Mountains of Alberta, Banff is one of Canada's more beautiful towns. A highlight of its summer is the Festival of the Arts. Students from the Banff Centre for Continuing Education, a world-famous school for the arts, show their skills by performing plays, ballets, operas, and classical concerts.

(opposite page) One Theatre Beyond Words production, **The Boy Who Could Sing Pictures,** *is about a young boy who grows up during medieval times. The performance uses puppets, masks, mime, and speaking parts to tell this exciting story.*

(right) The classic story of **Pinocchio** *comes to life center-stage at Toronto's Young People's Theatre. This theater has presented traditional and modern plays and musicals for young audiences and their families since opening its doors in 1966.*

(below) Elvis lives, or at least comes to life, with the help of the Famous People Players puppeteers.

Much of the television and film that Canadians watch is produced by Americans. Even though these television shows and movies are American-made, they are still "Canadian" in some ways. Many of the scenes are filmed in Canada's beautiful cities, mountains, and prairies!

Proudly Canadian

Canadian television networks realize the importance of showing programs that deal with national issues and provide Canadian role models. The government strongly supports the music, filmmaking, and television programming produced by Canadians. These industries are growing quickly, and Canadian productions are winning international awards for their excellent quality.

The CBC

The Canadian Broadcasting Corporation (CBC) is a very important part of Canadian culture. It is a government-owned network that provides radio and television broadcasting across Canada in both English and French. The CBC produces national news programs and documentaries as well as comedy and drama television programs.

Famous Canadian actors

You might be surprised to discover how many international celebrities are Canadian! Famous Hollywood faces include Michael J. Fox, John Candy, Catherine O'Hara, William Shatner, and Graham Green. News anchor Peter Jennings is Canadian, as is game-show host Alex Trebek.

(below) **Road to Avonlea** *is a weekly drama broadcast by the CBC. Based on the novels of Lucy Maud Montgomery, it looks at life in Prince Edward Island in the early 1900s. The main character, Sara Stanley, is played by Sarah Polley. This popular young actress also portrayed Ramona Quimby in a television series based on American author Beverly Cleary's "Ramona" books.*

(above) MuchMusic interviewer Natalie Richard chats with a member of a famous rock group. Passersby gather to watch the interview through the window. (right) Folk singer Bruce Cockburn is well known for his songs about the environment and other issues.

Music lovers

Canada is a nation of music lovers. Country, jazz, classical music, and rock are among the musical choices of Canadians. The music of different cultures, such as Jamaican reggae, African-American rap, Celtic folk music, and French-Canadian songs, has also become popular. Live music can be heard in crowded concert halls, stadiums, and night clubs across Canada.

MuchMusic

Young people particularly enjoy watching MuchMusic, a nationwide music television station. MuchMusic broadcasts videos, live performances, and personal interviews. It allows Canadian artists to become well known through their videos and guest appearances. MuchMusic also gives Canadian audiences a chance to become acquainted with the latest musical groups.

All that jazz

Canada's great jazz pianist, Oscar Peterson, has performed for audiences around the world. During his career, which spans more than 50 years, he has played with such great artists as Billie Holiday and Louis Armstrong. Peterson has received seven American Grammy Awards and numerous Canadian awards of recognition, including the Order of Canada. People continue to enjoy his jazz and blues music by listening to any of his 80 albums or by attending his concerts.

(above) This painting, called Sketch for the Jackpine, was painted by Tom Thomson. His paintings of northern Ontario's wilderness inspired the Group of Seven artists.
(left) Traditional skills, such as carving totem poles, are still practiced by many Native peoples. Artists also use weaving, printmaking, and embroidery to create Native art.
(below) Cornelius Krieghoff is well known for his colorful and realistic paintings of early French-Canadian settler life.

✿ Art in Canada ✿

An ancient art tradition

The wonders of nature have inspired Native artists for generations. Native arts range from the tall totem poles of the west-coast Haida to the eerie masks of the Iroquois. The Inuit skill of carving figures from soapstone is thousands of years old. Native artists still use traditional methods to express themselves in powerful and lasting ways.

Kane and Krieghoff

Among Canada's early settlers were artists who sketched scenes of pioneer life. Paul Kane journeyed across Canada with the Hudson's Bay Company canoe fleet. Along the way he painted pictures of the Native villages and huge herds of bison that wandered across the plains. Cornelius Krieghoff, a European painter who lived in Canada during the same period, recorded the life of the settlers living in Quebec.

The Group of Seven

Canada's most famous art was created in the 1920s by the Group of Seven. This band of painters, which eventually grew to include ten artists, portrayed the beauty of Canada's wilderness on canvas. These artists traveled throughout the land, capturing the spirit of every season in vivid colors and bold brush strokes. The Group of Seven artists were inspired by

Tom Thomson, a gifted artist who painted the wonders of northern Ontario. Unfortunately, Thomson died before the Group of Seven was formed. His paintings are similar in style to those of the Group of Seven, and his name is always associated with these artists.

William Kurelek

William Kurelek grew up on a farm in Alberta. As an adult, his paintings were influenced by his prairie roots, his Ukrainian upbringing, and his strong Christian faith. Kurelek created more than 1200 paintings of his childhood, which showed detailed scenes of everyday farm life.

Emily Carr

In the early twentieth century, Emily Carr recorded the vanishing Native villages, houses, and totem poles of British Columbia through her art. She also painted forests, skies, and beaches in a strong, colorful style. Carr's powerful paintings of her surroundings earned her the reputation of being one of Canada's great artists.

Art today

Art thrives in Canada. Galleries showing the works of today's artists, sculptors, and photographers can be found in every city. The art can range from realistic paintings to modern creations, such as the one shown below, which is Michael Snow's *Clothed Woman*.

✤ Buildings and structures ✤

Canada's cities and towns are made up of a blend of old and new architecture. As the country's population grew to include many cultures, building styles reflected the change. Over the last 50 years, many new buildings of glass and concrete have sprung up across Canada. They are marvels of modern design and technology.

The buildings of Toronto

Toronto, Canada's largest city, contains some amazing buildings. The CN Tower is the world's tallest free-standing structure. Every year, thousands of people take the elevator ride to the top of the tower to enjoy the spectacular view. Toronto's Skydome is the world's largest

stadium with a roof that opens and closes. This ultra-modern sports complex is 31-stories high and is home to the Toronto Blue Jays baseball team and the Toronto Argonauts football team. Toronto's City Hall consists of two curved buildings that stand out from the rectangular skyscrapers around them. This work of art was the winning design of a competition of architects hosted by the city.

(above) A spectacle of lights outlines Toronto's City Hall and the public skating rink in the foreground. (opposite) The West Edmonton Mall is the largest shopping center in the world! It houses a hotel, amusement parks, a zoo, and hundreds of stores.

A shopper's dream

The biggest attraction in the city of Edmonton, Alberta is the West Edmonton Mall. With over 800 stores, it is the world's largest shopping center. Adults and children can play in any of the mall's seven amusement parks, skate on the huge indoor ice rink, ride the fourteen-story-high roller coaster, or visit the sharks, dolphins, and other sea life at one of the aquariums. The West Edmonton Mall is filled with so many fun things to do that some visitors stay at its hotel and spend their entire vacation in the mall!

Ontario Science Centre

Where can you visit a tropical rainforest and see how a laser beam works all in one afternoon? If you answered "the Ontario Science Centre," you would be right. The Ontario Science Centre, located in Toronto, is a popular place for both children and adults. It offers many interesting hands-on exhibits and thrilling demonstrations. In the "Living Earth" display visitors can walk through a dark and damp cave or, with the help of special effects, experience how a hawk feels as it soars and swoops over the Niagara Escarpment.

A big birthday party

Every three to five years, great cities around the world hold international expositions, or world fairs. In 1967 Montreal was host to an exposition, or **expo**, called "Man and His World." In 1986 the city of Vancouver celebrated its 100th birthday with another expo. Many different countries participated by building amazing cultural pavilions and science-and-technology displays. One of the most eye-catching buildings on the expo site is Science World, formerly known as Expo Centre. This giant sphere is located right on the waterfront. It houses a movie theater and exhibits futuristic inventions.

National Gallery of Canada

The National Gallery of Canada in Ottawa is a blend of old and new architecture. It has an old-fashioned design but is built with modern materials. Glass walls, flower-filled gardens, and lofty ceilings give visitors the feeling of being outdoors. The National Gallery contains the best collection of Canadian and European art in Canada. It features Canadian works by such famous artists as Tom Thomson, Emily Carr, Cornelius Krieghoff, and the Group of Seven. European masterpieces painted by Rembrandt, Monet, and Rubens also hang on the gallery walls.

(above) The rainforest display is a popular part of the Ontario Science Centre's "Living Earth" exhibit. Many exotic varieties of plant life survive in a special room that is kept warm and humid. Visitors to the Centre can learn first-hand about this threatened part of the earth.

(right) The spectacular structure of the National Gallery is as much an example of art as the works displayed inside. Granite, wood, concrete, steel, and lots of glass have been combined in the building of this gallery. (below) The lights of Science World illuminate the Vancouver waterfront.

⚜ Sports ⚜

Not many people think of sports when they hear the word "culture," but sports are important to Canadian life. Hockey, lacrosse, and baseball are as much a part of culture as ballet!

Hockey

Ice hockey originated in Canada and is still Canada's most popular sport. In the 1850s, soldiers in Kingston, Ontario, invented this game using a lacrosse ball and field-hockey sticks. Later, players used a wooden disk or a cow's kneecap as a hockey puck! In 1875 the modern rules for hockey were developed, and the sport became very popular.

Canadians love hockey! Small cities and towns have local hockey teams, and larger cities have professional teams. A high point of the hockey season is the Stanley Cup playoffs. Professional hockey teams from across North America compete for the Stanley Cup, Canada's most famous trophy. Many great hockey players are Canadian heroes. Gordie Howe, Bobby Orr, Wayne Gretzky, and Mario Lemieux are examples.

Lacrosse

The game of lacrosse is based on *baggataway*, a game that was played by several Native groups. Playing *baggataway* was a good way of training warriors for battle because it tested their skills and endurance. Some games lasted for days, involved hundreds of people, and covered huge distances. Today a lacrosse team has ten players. Each carries a stick with a netted pocket, which is used to catch and fling a hard ball.

Baseball

Although baseball is usually considered an American sport, Canadians are enthusiastic fans of this exciting game. There are two major-league teams in Canada: the Montreal Expos and the Toronto Blue Jays. In 1992, people across Canada celebrated for several days when the Toronto Blue Jays won Canada's first World Series Championship. A huge parade took place in Toronto.

Canadian football

The Canadian Football League (CFL) was founded in 1958. Canadian football is similar to the American game, but the rules are slightly different. Every November the Grey Cup game determines the champion team. The players must often brave cold winds and snow to play this final game.

Curling

The object of curling is to slide a large smooth stone across an icy surface to a target. Curling was brought to Canada by Scottish immigrants, who found the long winters and plentiful ice perfect for this sport. Today Canadian curlers are among the world's best.

Skating

The sport of figure skating is a demanding one. Skaters perform a routine set to music, consisting of graceful gliding, spins, and jumps. The skaters are judged on the originality of their routines and skill of their moves. Many of Canada's figure skaters have won awards worldwide. Canada is also famous for its speedskaters, who zip around a circular rink at great speeds.

Rowing

Rowing regattas have taken place in Canada since 1818. Today, rowers take advantage of Canada's vast network of lakes, rivers, and ocean inlets to practice their sport. Rowing is one of Canada's strongest summer Olympic events. Canadian athletes have won awards in every rowing category.

(opposite page top) The National Hockey League, established in 1917, has grown from five Canadian teams to over 20 Canadian and American teams.
(center) One rowing event involves a crew of four rowers and one coxswain, who steers by calling the strokes and directing his or her teammates.
(bottom left) Lacrosse, one of Canada's oldest sports, is very popular among young athletes.
(bottom right) The Toronto Blue Jays jumped for joy when they won the 1992 World Series.

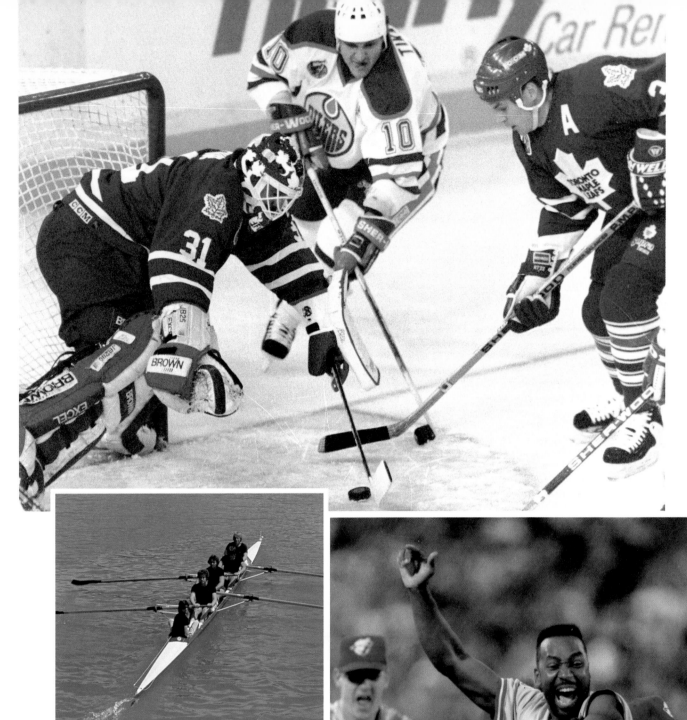

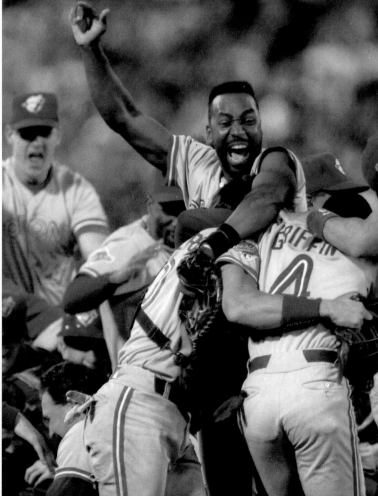

🍁 Celebrate Canada! 🍁

Write a fable

Read the Native legend on pages 6 and 7 and write a fable to explain one of nature's many mysteries. Use extraordinary characters and events. Start with one of these writing suggestions or come up with your own idea.

• All Canadian trees were green year round until, one autumn, a child artist dreamed of painting the leaves brilliant shades of yellow, orange, and red. How and why did the child's wish come true?

• Long ago, a young warrior who lived along the Niagara River told a lie so terrible that the riverbed cracked in two, and the water gushed forever over a great set of falls. Tell the story behind the warrior's lie and what the youth learned from the formation of Niagara Falls.

The marvelous maple leaf

In autumn, Canadian forests turn wonderful shades of red, orange, and yellow. The maple leaf, Canada's national symbol, is especially colorful. Write a poem, song, or short story that tells why you find Canada inspiring and copy the words onto a red, yellow, or brown construction-paper maple leaf. Encourage others to participate in this activity and work together to create an awesome autumn display for the walls of your classroom.

Mask making

Many of Canada's Native groups use masks in their traditional ceremonies. These masks represent supernatural beings. To design your own fanciful mask, begin by visiting the library to study a picture of a real Native mask. Once you have a design idea, open an old cereal box and lay it flat on a table. Sketch the mask shape onto the printed side and then cut out the mask. Using bold colors of paints or markers, design a face on the blank side of the cardboard. Use masking tape to attach a handle made of a ruler or a piece of scrap wood to your mask so that you can hold it in front of your face.

Cross-cultural school fair

Canadian students come from a variety of cultural backgrounds. They make their schools lively by sharing their different cultural traditions with one another. Is your student body made up of many cultures? If so, organize a cross-cultural school fair to celebrate the heritage of your fellow students. The fair might include ethnic food stalls, artwork displays from different countries, a global fashion show, and folk-dance performances. Draw a world map and attach it to a bulletin board. Mark each student's home country or the country of his or her ancestors with a small flag pin.

Carving a tradition

Long ago, an ivory polar bear, a soapstone lamp, and a child's wooden toy might have been among an Inuit family's treasures. The ability to carve was a necessary skill. Today Inuit artists continue this tradition by using a variety of materials. To create an Inuit-style sculpture, use a plant-rooting substance called Vermiculite, plaster-of-paris, an old toothbrush, and paint.

Place two large cupfuls of plaster-of-paris in an old plastic margarine container with one cupful of Vermiculite. Add water and stir the mixture until it looks like thick porridge without any lumps. Leave the plaster to harden for a couple of days. When it is dry, turn the margarine container over and pop out the hardened plaster. Use a dull dinner knife to carve your sculpture. When your carving is done, paint the sculpture white, then splatter it with darker paint by running your fingernail across the paint-filled bristles of the brush. Your finished sculpture will look like real stone.

Trivial pursuit

The world-famous "Trivial Pursuit" board game was invented by four fact-loving Canadians. Use this book and other books about Canada to create your own trivia question cards and game board. Invite your friends and family to play.

 **Truly Canadian**

The Royal Canadian Mounted Police

Canada is well known for its peaceful cities and law-abiding citizens. This reputation for honesty is partly due to the national law-enforcement agency called the Royal Canadian Mounted Police (RCMP). Traditionally, "Mounties" dressed in scarlet uniforms and wide-brimmed Stetson hats were famous for bringing to justice such colorful criminals as the Mad Trapper of Rat River. Today the red outfits are worn only on ceremonial occasions such as the famous **Musical Ride**. People come from around the world to watch this colorful parade of Mounties on horseback. As the music plays, the horses move through complicated formations. In their daily work, RCMP officers patrol the borders and coastlines, police the highways, and provide law enforcement throughout Canada.

Canada's national anthem

O CANADA

O Canada!
  Our home and native land!
True patriot love
  in all thy sons command.
With glowing hearts
  we see thee rise,
The True North
  strong and free!
From far and wide,
  O Canada,
We stand on guard
  for thee.
God keep our land
  glorious and free!
O Canada,
  we stand on guard for thee.
O Canada,
  we stand on guard for thee!

Ô CANADA

Ô Canada
  Terre de nos aïeux,
Ton front est ceint
  de fleurons glorieux!
Car ton bras
  sait porter l'épée,
Il sait porter
  la croix!
Ton histoire
  est une épopée
Des plus
  brillants exploits,
Et ta valeur,
  de foi trempée,
Protégera nos foyers
  et nos droits,
Protégera nos foyers
  et nos droits.

🩰 Glossary 🩰

acrobat A person skilled in performing feats such as walking on a tightrope

ancestor A person from whom one is descended

architecture The science, art, or profession of designing, planning, and constructing buildings and other structures

Arctic The region surrounding the North Pole

audition A short performance that tests the abilities of a singer, dancer, or other performer

culture The customs, beliefs, and arts of a distinct group of people

documentary A program or film that deals with or gives facts and information on a particular subject

elder A senior member of a Native group

folk dance A dance that originated among the common people of a certain region or country

heritage The customs, achievements, and history passed on from earlier generations

illuminate To light up

immigrant A person who settles in a new country

Inuit Native people who live in Canada's Arctic

Iroquois A confederation of Native nations in southeastern Ontario and southern Quebec

jig A fast, lively dance

legend A story passed down through the years

medieval Describing the time period in Europe from about 395 AD to 1500 AD

Niagara Escarpment The cliff region around the Niagara River in southern Ontario

Order of Canada The highest Canadian award given for special achievements

physiotherapist A person who treats injuries or diseases with methods such as massage or exercise

playwright A person who writes plays

rainforest A dense forest in an area of high rainfall

regatta A boat race

skyscraper A very tall building

traditions Long-held customs or beliefs

trapeze A short, swinging horizontal bar suspended from two ropes

🩰 Index 🩰

1 2 3 4 5 6 7 8 9 0 Printed in the U.S.A. 2 1 0 9 8 7 6 5 4 3